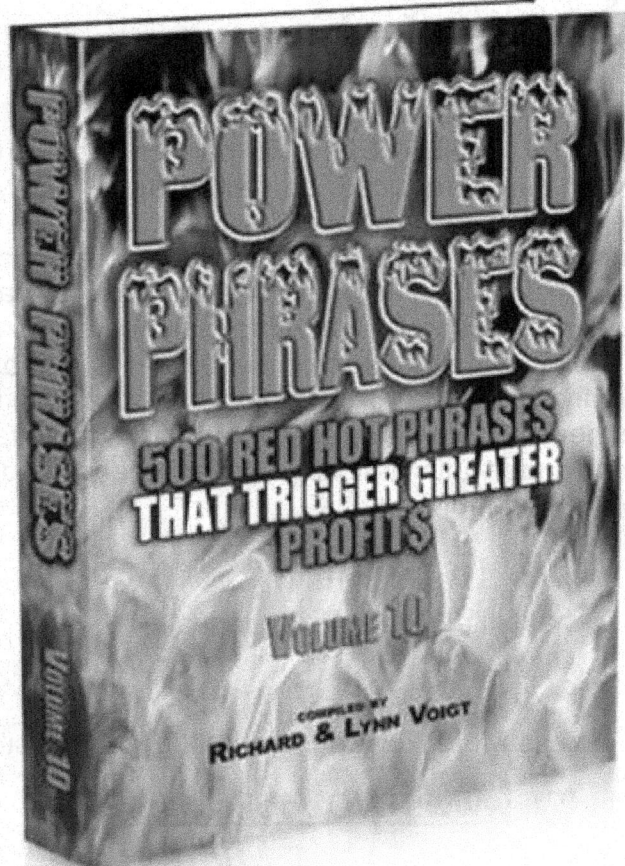

POWER PHRASES

500 RED HOT PHRASES THAT TRIGGER GREATER PROFITS

Volume 10

COMPILED BY
RICHARD & LYNN VOIGT

POWER PHRASES – Vol. 10
500 Power Phrases That Trigger Greater Profits

First Printing, 2013

Printed in the United States of America

To Access More Powerful Marketing Tools Visit:

www.RIVObooks.com

www.RIVOinc.com

www.WisconsinGarden.com

Income Disclaimer

This book contains educational materials meant to inspire ways to promote personal ideas, products and services that may be appropriate to incorporate or use in one's personal or business strategy, marketing method or any other related personal or business, that regardless of the author's results and experience, may not produce the same results (or any results) for you. The authors make absolutely no guarantee, either expressed or implied, that by implementing any ideas herein will gain success, make money, or improve current personal or business circumstances. There are simply far too many variable factors that come into play regarding any level of achievement or success in said personal and/or business venture. Primarily, results will depend on the nature of the product or business model, the conditions of the marketplace, the experience of the individual, and situations and elements that are beyond your control or that of the authors.

As with any business endeavor, you assume all risk related to investment and money based on your own discretion and at your own potential expense. If you intend to quote, copy, or use any content herein, in part or whole, it shall be the sole responsibility of the individual to be mindful of all active and lawfully protected copyrights, trademarks, and/or services-marks, by conducting due diligence prior to said usage.

Liability Disclaimer

This book is strictly intended for educational purposes only and was intended to inspire the individual to create ideas of their own design. This book represents the views of the authors as of the date of publication. Due to constant changing conditions facing the information age, the authors reserve the irrevocable right to modify and update their opinions based upon changing conditions. While the authors have made a "good faith" effort to verify the accuracy of information within this book, the authors or their affiliates/partners do not assume any liability or responsibility for inadvertent errors, omissions, or inaccuracies. This book is not intended to be used as a legal guide or resource, nor are the authors attempting to render any legal, accounting, theraputic, medical, or other professional services or advice. If said professional consultation or adivce is required, the authors recommend the reader immediately seek the services of a competent professional. It shall be the reader's responsibility to be fully aware of any and all federal, state, local or country laws that govern and/or affect personal or business transactions. Any slight of ethnicity, culture, gender, orientation, or existing organization as is any reference to persons or businesses, living or dead, is unintentional and purely coincidental.

Terms of Use

You are given a non-transferable, "personal use" license to this book. You cannot distribute it or share it with other individuals. Also, there are no resale rights or private label rights granted when purchasing this book. In other words, it's for your own personal use only.

POWER PHRASES

Vol. 10

500 POWER PHRASES THAT TRIGGER GREATER PROFITS

-·|·-•·*”""*·•·-|·-•**•-·|·-•·*”’’’*·•-·|·-

Compiled by

Richard & Lynn Voigt
I.M. Education Specialists

Introduction: Pro Edition 5000 Power Phrases

Powerful Phrases, Headlines, Sub Headlines, Slogans, Bullet Points and Interview Sound Bites are perhaps the most powerful marketing tools mankind has ever created. They are the lifeblood behind every business venture are the ultimate secret weapon of Millionaire Marketers.

No matter whether you are introducing or promoting a brand new product, teaching a "How To" skill, building a website, or simply sending an email, using the perfect power phrase is crucial to capturing and holding eyeballs and producing greater marketing profits.

In today's world every word you use has measurable impact. Each word can produce emotional psychological buttons that trigger psychological reactions. Successful advertisers understand that using an effective power phrase is a true art form that turns "wants" into instant gratification "needs." Once artfully triggered, any niche market can instantly create more protifable conversions.

Now it's your turn to personalize this incredible collection of 5000 Power Phrases in ways that instantly advance your own effective marketing skills as you create new and power phrases, slogans, presentations, bullet points, or interview sound bites that take you to the next level.

Whether starting or running a small business, writing an ad, coming up with a memorable slogan, making a major corporate presentation, bullet points, creating a video, writing a book, searching for the perfect slogan, teaching a lesson or book report, your creative use of these Power Phrases can capture more eyeballs and produce some amazing rewards quickly turning you into a Marketing Genius. Now, it's your turn to make the magic happen!

POWER PHRASES

Vol. 10 – 4501 - 5000

500 Power Phrases That Trigger Greater Profits

Begin Selecting & Customizing Your Perfect Marketing Phrase

4501	Rest And Relax
4502	Start Winning Today
4503	So This Is What I'm Going To Do To Help
4504	Go Ahead, Make My Data!
4505	Two Biggest Challenges Beginners Face
4506	Establish Your Pre-Eminence
4507	All It Takes Is A Little Bit Of Elbow Grease
4508	Share The Story
4509	Imagination Is Your Greatest Opportunity
4510	Make Marketing Your Top Priority
4511	It Has Everything To Do With You
4512	You Can Change Your Mind
4513	Think Back To How Life Felt Before This
4514	Catch This Business Opportunity While It's Hot
4515	First Question
4516	Common Ways To Die Quickly Online
4517	The Real Sinister Side Of Failed Continuity
4518	New Trend Brewing
4519	Nice Power And Influence
4520	Overcoming Writer's Block
4521	There's No Other Way To Succeed

4522	Most People Don't Know This
4523	Marketing And Sales Aren't 2nd Class Jobs
4524	Final Words Of Encouragement
4525	Why We're Unique
4526	Failure Is Schooling
4527	Works Like Viagra For Your Campaigns
4528	Play Catch With Cash Anytime
4529	What's Your New Direction
4530	We All Go Through This
4531	How Real Can It Get
4532	Claim Your Role
4533	Advanced Notice
4534	Snafu Disasters
4535	Ask Quality Questions Receive Quality Answers
4536	Smart Marketers Are Taking Notice
4537	The Marketing Effect On Our Environment
4538	Every Crunch Helps
4539	Start Spreading Light
4540	Find Out How Much Real Advertisers Are Paying
4541	Upload Your Future
4542	Time To Quit That Sucky Day Job
4543	Magnetize Your Efforts
4544	Guess Who's Figuring This Out
4545	You Don't Need All Of This Stuff
4546	In The Space Of Just THREE Years
4547	First Contact
4548	The Why What How And What If
4549	The Message Mess
4550	Check Out My Facebook Profile
4551	The Truth Is It's Too Unrealistic
4552	Together We Will Create An Incredible Team Of Experts
4553	Rethink Your Links
4554	Friendly World Class Customer Support
4555	This Solved My Problem
4556	My Misfortune Is Your Luck
4557	Open A Store For Peanuts
4558	They're Always Looking For People Who Get It
4559	Post Holiday Deals

4560	Leave Your Comfort Zone Cocoon
4561	Use My Fulfillment Center
4562	What New Marketers Need To Know About Advertising Effectively
4563	I Bet You Made This Mistake
4564	Random Zig Zag Patterns
4565	Ingenious Prospecting System
4566	See Cash In Days From Now On
4567	Looking For The Best Of The Best
4568	I'll Start Building Your Business Today
4569	Let The Rest Of The World Know
4570	Feel Guilty About Taking This From Me
4571	Break Into Any Niche
4572	Your Final Frontier
4573	Preponderance Of Proof
4574	Looking For An Easier Way To Get Started
4575	Shift Of Interest
4576	Don't Eye F... The Camera
4577	The One Last Place
4578	Incredible Storewide Savings
4579	What's In Store For Your Future
4580	Reputation Created Demand
4581	Stop Making Your Boss Rich
4582	Feeling Overwhelmed Perhaps This Is What You Need
4583	Tiny Time Capsule
4584	Have You Ever Been Up This Situation
4585	Don't Be Left Out
4586	The Day's Recap
4587	Pushes You In Just The Right Way
4588	Pay Per Play Video Ads
4589	Stifle Unplugged
4590	What Do You Collectively Know
4591	Keep The Background Simple
4592	What Branding Can Do For You
4593	Change Your Resolution
4594	Engagement Driven Copywriting
4595	Make Money Passively
4596	You Can See What I Mean
4597	It's Paying Off In Green

4598	Selling Has Little To Do With Slick Ads
4599	I Missed You
4600	As Soon As You Click
4601	Inner Circle Programs
4602	Self Improvement Priority
4603	$1,980 With No Selling
4604	Make A To-Do List
4605	There Simply Is No Limit
4606	Mastering Your Body Language
4607	A New Buzz Phrase Is Just Reaching The Internet
4608	Come Back Tomorrow And This Offer May Be Gone
4609	Concerned About Your Finances
4610	Finding The Power Source
4611	Here Is Just Some Of What You Can Do
4612	The Pressure Is Off
4613	The Manifestation Of Social Order
4614	Punishment & Examination Destroys
4615	How To Cut Credit Card Payments In Half
4616	Get Unfrazzled
4617	Buy New Products That Add To Your Life
4618	Watch The People Popping Out Of The Woodwork
4619	She Hates This
4620	Jump Start Your Brain
4621	Let The Soil Be Your Canvas
4622	Converting Faith Into Results
4623	Why Do So Many People Fail
4624	Best Option Is To Compress It
4625	Create More Profits Than An Internet Slot Machine
4626	Are You Always Sending Something Useful
4627	Click And Convert Cash In No Time
4628	Cash Building Strategies
4629	Let's Play More Video Games
4630	Why Success Happens 20X Faster Today
4631	Customers Will Be Telling You Want They Need
4632	The Women With The Midas Touch
4633	How To Get Rich
4634	Learn To Earn
4635	You've Been Flagged

4636	Control Trial Expiration Dates
4637	Capture Their Attention More Than Once
4638	What's Your Perception Of Reality
4639	Is This For Sale In Your Territory
4640	Pick Up Your Empire And Move
4641	Stick With This For One Minute
4642	Commitment + Perseverance + Opportunity = Failure
4643	Where Incentives Work
4644	Customer Acquisition Costs
4645	I'm Going To Beat You No Matter What
4646	Now's Your Chance
4647	Being Natural Convinces More People
4648	You Have The Power To Create Amazing Profits
4649	Smiling Along The Way
4650	End Low Project Morale
4651	Ferocious Debate
4652	Make The Assumption
4653	Your Compensation
4654	Affirm You're The Best Marketer In The Universe
4655	Through Them Bizarre And Unusual Questions
4656	Have You Ever Wondered Why Your Computer Runs So Slowly
4657	Piggy Back On This
4658	Perfecting Relationships
4659	Let's See How You Handle This
4660	Stop Buying Expensive Lead Lists Today
4661	Entitlement vs. Enlightenment
4662	Stop The Money Leak
4663	Tricky Timepieces
4664	This Is An Experiment
4665	Powerful Anchor Points Generate Conversions
4666	Never Been Done Before
4667	Most People Are Never Listened To Let Alone Heard
4668	Respect Their Time
4669	It's All About Trade Offs
4670	Never Send A Lifeless Impersonal Message Again
4671	How To Get Started The Right Way
4672	Test Website Fonts
4673	Why Type Of Product Do People Pay The Most For

4674	The Most Expensive Item In The World
4675	Are Powerful Advertising Techniques Merely A Myth
4676	How About A Whole New Approach To Internet Marketing
4677	Is Your Website On Life Support
4678	I'm Not Removing You Just Yet
4679	Break Through Your Financial Freedom Ceiling
4680	Use These Techniques
4681	The Future Internet Weapon
4682	This Company's On Fire
4683	Build Some Buzz Around It
4684	Your Rat Race Escape Plan
4685	Linking Like A Millionaire
4686	Putting Everyone In Earshot Of Your Marketing Campaign
4687	If Network Campaigns Are So Great Why Haven't You Joined
4688	Inexpensive Video Tips Tools And Techniques
4689	Let's Make The Best Possible
4690	Freedom In An Unfree World
4691	Showcase Your Proposed Specialty
4692	A Great Mentor Is Your Career Doctor
4693	My Cash Empire Is Now Exposed
4694	Rapidly Changing Publishing Landscape
4695	Our Job Is To Succeed
4696	Learn More Right Now - Click Here
4697	Your Headline Brings Them In
4698	Did You Know The 4 Learning Styles
4699	How To Quickly Evaluate A Real Business Opportunity
4700	Now That You've Got It - Keep It Going
4701	Excited & Awestruck No Wonder Why
4702	Up Front And Center
4703	Link Away
4704	Written Video Instructions
4705	What Are You Doing
4706	Higher Chance Of Divorce
4707	This Should Be Your Sounding Board
4708	Large Margin Profits
4709	Significant Approach
4710	B Is For Blogging Your Passion
4711	Great Way For Newbies To Start

4712	Smile While You Sleep
4713	People Don't Look At Crappy Headlines
4714	How Fast Do You Want To Make Money
4715	Great Low Prices Where Affiliates Are Welcome
4716	What Does Your Prospect Really Want
4717	Wicked Is The Word
4718	Why Most Niche Ideas Aren't Good
4719	Rebranding To Increase Sales
4720	GPS Your Own Roadmap To Wealth
4721	Tune In Your Marketing Taste Buds
4722	You Can Try It Out For 30 Days For Free
4723	Habits vs. Destiny
4724	Can't Get Rolling
4725	True Motivation
4726	Effective Ways To Reduce Your Business Costs
4727	Little Money Coming In More Going Out
4728	Do It Yourself Marketing On A Budget
4729	Instant Access To Shocking New Videos
4730	Make Money From Online
4731	Customers Like The Same Face
4732	Is Money A Weakness
4733	The One Easiest To Produce
4734	The Power Of Heroism
4735	How To Look Great On Camera
4736	Improve Your Aim
4737	February Commission Payment
4738	Turn Little Splashes Into Humongous Floods
4739	Revoking User Access
4740	Something Special For Everyone
4741	Let Them Do It All
4742	Look Upward To The Camera
4743	Focused Content I Can Trust
4744	Still Relying On Couch Surfing
4745	Category Launches
4746	It Works On Everyone
4747	It Usually Doesn't Work Out That Way
4748	It Doesn't Matter When Your Headline Sucks
4749	Does Your Child Ever Embarrass You

4750	Plan Of Action
4751	Everybody Will Lose Their Job
4752	Easiest Way Toward Marketing Success
4753	Buzz Surrounding A Highly Anticipated Release
4754	Much Easier Than You Think
4755	Which Approach Would You Rather Take
4756	Why Would We Look Forward To Helping You Make Money
4757	Effective Selling Really Is About Getting Anybody To Do Anything
4758	Bucketing Money
4759	Just Real Traffic
4760	The Power Of The Moment
4761	Let Me Tell You A Little About It Right Now
4762	Legitimate Business Opportunity Leads For Free
4763	What's Worse Than A Hiccup
4764	The Secret Headline That Always Works
4765	Create Your Own Personal Morning Ritual
4766	Start Laughing All The Way To The Bank
4767	Digital Marketing
4768	Responsible For Tons Of Conversions
4769	Still Trudging Through The Internet Swamp
4770	Get On The Phone And Start Talking To Them Personally
4771	That's Just Crazy To Me
4772	Wet Their Appetite
4773	What The Keys To Your Kingdom
4774	Ever Consider Name Dropping
4775	List At Least 5 Benefits
4776	Activate A Relentless Vision
4777	I Wouldn't Risk It Not Anymore
4778	How To Become Miss Information Or Answerman
4779	It's Also Quite Expensive But
4780	100% Commission On Every Sale
4781	Back To You Lynn
4782	Your Marketing Lookout Tower
4783	Get Your Daily Alert
4784	Posts By Category
4785	Have Fun With This
4786	Shifting Through Available Information
4787	Billions Up For Grabs

4788	We Know We Look Good
4789	Before Moving Forward
4790	Member To Member Payments
4791	Debt Drink And Drugs
4792	Texting In The Shade
4793	Confidence Is A Choice
4794	Write Your Own Paychecks Every Day
4795	The Red Light Challenge
4796	Walking Out On A Horrible Boss
4797	Time To Infuse The Power
4798	Blogging For Dollars
4799	Richard RIVO Interviews
4800	Liberating Financial Freedom
4801	The Scarcity Must Be Real
4802	I Worked Hard For Over 40 Years
4803	Free Overnight Shipping
4804	Go Where The Money Is
4805	How To Earn Money
4806	I've Got The Product If You've Got The Traffic
4807	The Price Stake Out
4808	We Don't Want To Waste A Lot Of Money
4809	Fulfilling Dreams Takes Money
4810	Win Advancement
4811	When The Truth Starts Hurting
4812	7 Social Network Profiles
4813	Site Targeting
4814	Get Mesmerized Visitors
4815	Log Into The Membership Site
4816	It Takes 200 People To Deliver This
4817	This Is Your Watershed Moment
4818	Great Headlines Generate Sales Every Second
4819	Ambition And Achievement
4820	On The Spot
4821	You Think This Is The Best Offer You've Ever Seen
4822	It's Not For Over-Thinkers
4823	Why I Used To Be Broke
4824	Sharing My Strategies From The Stage
4825	Cold Conversions Reheating Up

4826	Cascades Of Cash
4827	Can't Say Thank You Enough
4828	Deliver Quality To Targeted Prospects
4829	No Guess Work Involved
4830	Is Your Consumer Always In Charge
4831	Headlines That Grab A Reader's Attention
4832	All I'm Trying To Do Is Get It Right
4833	Roll With Your Imperfections
4834	Open Your Presents
4835	Tell Your Boss Goodbye
4836	I Hate When People Fail Online
4837	Easiest Business Model On Earth
4838	Experience A Fantastic Conversion Rate
4839	How To Get 'Em Done Fast
4840	Post Your Free Ad Right Now
4841	Fast Simple Budget Friendly
4842	A Wide Range Of Nets
4843	Following Up On The Auto Follow Disaster
4844	Unconscious Signals That Distract
4845	Pretty Good vs. Highly Productive
4846	Get Expert Help
4847	Why They Dream About It
4848	Buckaroos Are Back
4849	Switch It Up
4850	It's Better If It's Not Perfect
4851	Hook Them In
4852	The Mind Has To Answer
4853	It's All About Precise Planning For Financial Success
4854	Testing New Killer Karaoke
4855	You'll Never Be Poor Again
4856	Whiff Of Irony
4857	One Of Earth's Greatest Treasures
4858	The Thinking Brain Likes Power
4859	What's The Difference Between McDonalds And Coca Cola
4860	Prepare For The Affiliate War
4861	Stay Tuned For Complete Details
4862	Acting Decisively
4863	Scared Of New Heights

4864	Google Flags Coming
4865	Stand Up And Demand Success
4866	Discover The Angles
4867	How To Set Up The Ultimate Marketing System
4868	Your Book Can Effectively Change Lives
4869	Don't Stop Now
4870	What I'm Trying To Say
4871	Move On To What Works
4872	St. Nick Pick
4873	You'll Have Full Product Resell Rights
4874	So Don't Delay Secure YOUR Place Today
4875	Watch Your List Start Growing Like Crazy
4876	You Need Their Commitment That They Want It
4877	Solid Colors Tend To Work Best
4878	Category Personal
4879	Never Have To Owe Anyone
4880	Here Are Some Video Examples
4881	Save BIG I Mean Huge
4882	Business Home Internet Marketing Opportunity
4883	Most Fall Flat On Their Face
4884	Build Your Own Safelist Starting Right Now
4885	Help Yourself Generate A Full Time Income
4886	Scanners Speed Read
4887	Reap The Benefits
4888	Unused Knowledge Means Nothing
4889	Sleek Sexy Rockets
4890	Decide What To Make
4891	Resume Sites Offer Better Service Results
4892	Why I'm So Thankful
4893	What's The One Thing You Do Best
4894	Want To Sell Your Music CDs
4895	Call Today To Secure Your Seat
4896	Categorically Boost My Response
4897	Once You Sign Up
4898	Learn How To Create A Winning Mindset
4899	Advanced Word Marketing Tactics That Work
4900	Incremental Innovation Markets
4901	Take Your Free Position Right Away

16

4902	Things Too Costly
4903	Simple Way Google Made Us #1
4904	Building Up Your Skills
4905	No Jumping Through Hoops
4906	Websites Die From Lack Of Sales
4907	Security Is Paramount But Content Is King
4908	Listen To Your Intuition
4909	It's Not My Thing - It's Their Thing
4910	Careful Who You Sit Next To
4911	A Niche Is A Living Breathing Entity
4912	We've Learned Our Lessons The Hard Way So Listen Up
4913	You Need To Hear This
4914	Building A Support System
4915	Turn You Messes Into A Message
4916	Get Paid First
4917	5 Biggest Reasons Why I Should Buy Your Product Or Service
4918	Trust And Inspire Yourself
4919	What Value Do You Provide
4920	Are You Hiding Behind Your Computer
4921	Now You Can Get What You Really Want
4922	Perfecting The Process
4923	This Isn't The Next Fad - It's Here To Stay
4924	Staring At A Blank Monitor
4925	How Badly Did You Always Want This
4926	First Thanks For Purchasing My Course
4927	Where Insecurity And Fears Reside
4928	Generate Immediate Cash With This Product
4929	This Year's Hottest Offer
4930	Are You Sitting Down For This
4931	The Joy Of Collaboration
4932	The Answer Would Be Priceless
4933	What Can You Do That's Different From Your Competition
4934	Here's What Really Happened
4935	Stuff You Already Know How To Do
4936	Get Ultra Focused
4937	Working For Yourself Is Addictive
4938	Lest I Forget
4939	Alternative Approach From Failure To Success

4940	How White And Black Disrupt Video
4941	Cut Out The Marketing Middleman
4942	Today We're All In The Art Business
4943	Updating Your Email Preferences
4944	Disinvent Failure
4945	Being With People You Need
4946	Money Tools To Bank On
4947	Action Generates Reaction
4948	Without Directly Spilling The Milk
4949	Please Don't Hesitate To Call Us
4950	Fall In Love With Your Work
4951	You Can't Put A Price On Truth
4952	Start College Funds For Your Children
4953	Major Core Strategies
4954	Grab An Arsenal Of Adrenaline
4955	Keep All The Money You Collect
4956	Getting The Best Possible Results
4957	My Best Marketing Strategy Unveiled
4958	Score Higher With Original Content
4959	Break Solutions Into 3 Action Steps
4960	Send Your Traffic Into Hyperdrive
4961	Highly Paid Marketing Consultant
4962	Avoid The Temptation Of Being Distracted
4963	This Will Change Your Business And Life Forever
4964	Don't Do That - Let It Go
4965	Best Return Of Investment In Marketing Comes From Testing
4966	How Are You Using Your Booster Stations
4967	Eliminate All Possibilities Of Miscommunication
4968	Internal Scoring That Destroys Our Self Confidence
4969	Developing Courage
4970	Budget Friendly
4971	Will You Be Wearing A Mic
4972	What's Coming Across
4973	The Voice In The Back Of Your Head
4974	Learn How To Move
4975	Things Are Getting Serious
4976	People Buy Anything If The Price Is Right
4977	Would You Work For Yourself As An Employer

4978	Outlining All The Key Steps
4979	Search Engine Optimization Is Key To Your Success Online
4980	Make Subheads Bigger In A Different Font
4981	The Shipping Is On Us
4982	Opinions Are Like Lips
4983	Pursuing Market Share Over Profit
4984	I Really Want To Hear About Problems
4985	Think Carefully About Your Decision
4986	Motion vs. Emotion
4987	Soul To Soul Communications
4988	Knocking Down Your Door Wanting
4989	Know The Rules
4990	You Never Know How Strong You Are Until
4991	48-Hour Exclusive Coupon
4992	Why 99% Of Programs Are Complete Outright Scams
4993	Working Together We All Win
4994	Skip The Mistakes Most People Make
4995	Why They're Moving In This Direction
4996	Behavioral Marketing
4997	Evaluate Progress And Success Of Your Marketing
4998	Ninja Cash Tactics
4999	Is Anybody Out There
5000	I Await Your Response

Lynn and I hope that this "Think Tank" Pro Edition complete volume series of 5000 Hot Phrases will helped you clearly paint your dreams, sell your ideas, and market your messages, propelling each of your ideas and projects toward incredible success.

We truly wish you the very best and look forward to hearing your success stories.

Concluding Thoughts:

Ever success is built upon a preparing a strong foundation, having a clear vision, and taking positive action each and every day. If you've been searching for a new lifestyle, then you'll find this book directive and inspirational. You can open it to any page and let that page help you rethink possibilities, consider new ideas, open new opportunities, and ultimately experience a more successful and fulfilling lifestyle.

Every problem has a solution! Regardless of your current situation or circumstance, know that you have the power and responsibility to redirect your life in any direction you choose. Simply start thinking about and research the kind of lifestyle that truly appeals to your heart. Begin your new journey by learning everything you can about your chosen subject. When you make that commitment, you'll open more unexpected doors to unique opportunities than imagined.

"Creative Thought Is The Only Reality
Everything Else Is Merely The By-Product Of That Thought."
- Walter Russell

So why not start thinking **BIGGER? It won't cost you any more.** It all starts by never allowing your current life's situation, environment, or so-called friends to limit your path to a happier, healthier, and successful life. After all, whose life is this?

Make a decision to focus on learning something new each and every day. Begin attracting your ideal lifestyle by doing something you love and enjoy. As difficult as it may be, don't allow money to limit your dreams. Focus on the kind of thoughts that make you feel good. Once you learn how to control your focus, you'll have a great chance to see your dreams take shape. You've finally learn to harness the power you always had within, a Universal Energy stream that flows 365/24/7 in any direction your project your thoughts, Good or Bad. Want proof? The thoughts you currently believe and project reflect the life you're currently living. Therefore, if your life isn't happening, change your thoughts, and change your life. It's something only you can hold, visualize, and project, living your dream come true.

Find yourself a mentor and spend more time with people who truly appreciate, support, and foster your dreams. Life may be short, but the thoughts we hold can make our life wider and more fulfilling.

20

About The Authors:

Richard and Lynn develop creative strategies that paint dreams, sell ideas, & market messages   Together, they present a unique team-approach, working side-by-side, helping clients pursue their passions while sharing their skills and diverse expertise as authors, artists, inventors, entrepreneurs, & Internet marketing education specialists.

Teaching by example, they mentor proven self-publishing services, graphic design, video production, domain acquisition, and marketing research of behalf of their company, RIVO Inc – RIVO Marketing, since 1997. They've created & produced hundreds of videos, self-published dozens of books on a wide variety of topics and created thousands of original works of fine art, while refining their Internet Marketing techniques, mentoring programs, and related business website development.

Their mission is to continually uncover new products and services, test new strategies, and network useful solutions with off and online entrepreneurs, small business owners, writers, local artists, models, teachers, students, and marketing professionals.

Their goal is to help clients create an action plan that discovers and connects the missing pieces of the success puzzle. The goals they foster create multiple streams of income for today's volatile economic climate. Their motto is: "Do the work once and allow the work to create additional streams of income for a lifetime."

Feel free to contact them if you have questions or would like to tap into their talents and expertise. They appreciate your feedback and look forward to hearing your success stories.

Contact:
Richard & Lynn Voigt - RIVO
I. M. Education Specialists

RIVO INC - RIVO Marketing
13720 West Keefe Avenue
Brookfield, Wisconsin 53005 – USA
Email: support@RIVOinc.com
Website: www.RIVObooks.com
Website: www.WisconsinGarden.com

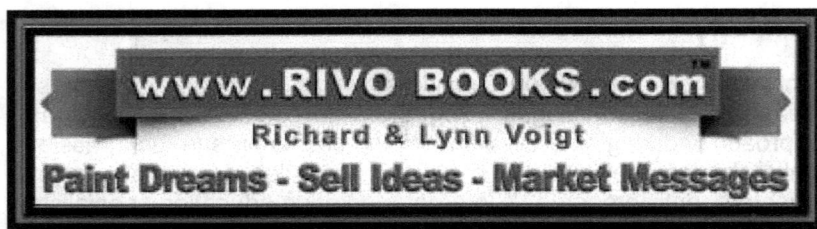

Visit Lynn's Garden: www.WisconsinGarden.com
view hundreds of great garden video blogs Tips

See Richard's Unique Artwork: www.RIVOart.com
view over 3,000 original Fine-Art compositions

Our Book Titles Now Available On Amazon:

THE GOLDEN VAULT OF MOTIVATIONAL QUOTATIONS
Words of Wisdom from The Greatest Minds & Leaders

BABY NAME .ME - 21,400 Names & Nicknames
For Family, Friends, Pets, Natural & Man-Objects

DOODLE DESIGNS Volumes 1-3
For Professionals & Kids Of All Ages
DOODLE DESIGNS – Vol. 1
DOODLE DESIGNS – Vol. 2
DOODLE DESIGNS Coloring Book Vol. 3

Work MORE Accomplish LESS Get FIRED!

ACTION HEADLINES That Drive Emotions – Volumes 1- 6
Paint Dreams, Sell Ideas & Market Your Message
Action Headlines That Drive Emotions Vol. 1
Action Headlines That Drive Emotions Vol. 2
Action Headlines That Drive Emotions Vol. 3
Action Headlines That Drive Emotions Vol. 4
Action Headlines That Drive Emotions Vol. 5
Action Headlines That Drive Emotions Vol. 6

IDIOMS – IDIOMS - IDIOMS
6,450 Popular Expressions That Put Words In Your Mouth

The CLICHÉ BIBLE - 8,400 Clichés For Sports Fanatics
& Lovers Of Popular Expressions

MORE THAN WORDS
5000+ Marketing Phrases That Sell

HYPNOTIC PHRASING
WARNING-This Book Teaches You How To Grab Eyeballs

YOUR RIGHT TO WEALTH
Becoming Wealthy Isn't Hard When You Know How

WI GARDEN – Let's Get Dirty
Our Wisconsin Garden Guide Promoting Delicious, Healthier Home-Grown Fresh Food, With Tools, Tips, & Ideas That Inspire Gardeners!

MONETIZE YOUR SOCIAL LIFE
Earn Extra Income While Having Fun Online

BABY NAMES
21,400 Unique Baby Names & Nicknames

FUNNY HEADLINES vol. 1
3,500 Outrageous Silly Brain Toots

FUNNY HEADLINES vol. 2
3,500 Outrageous Silly Brain Toots

JOBS
10,240 Career Paths That Can Change Your Life!

MONEY WORDS
Powerful Phrases That Million Dollar Copywriters Use To Make Piles Of Cash On Demand!

GARDEN QUOTATIONS
400 Garden Quotes From The Earth To Your Soul

HEADLINE STARTERS
175,000 Words That Paint Dreams, Sell Ideas, And Market Your Message

BABY NAMES
25,350 Baby Names & Nicknames For Your Family Friends & Pets
    697 pages 7,000 Names with Origin & Meaning plus Top 100 Names, And 2,000 Most Popular Names

CURIOUS WORDS
15,800 Words That Expand Your Mind And Change Your Life

INSPIRING THOUGHTS
That Inspire Happiness, Success & A Clearer Understanding Of Life

MARKETING EYEBALLS
100 Ideas That Can Add Unlimited Subscribers To Your Lists

SECOND OF FIVE
My Early Years- From Birth To High School

POWER PHRASES – Individual Volumes 1 - 10
500 Power Phrases That Trigger Greater Profits

POWER PHRASES Pro Edition – (Complete Series Volumes 1-10)
5000 Power Phrases That Trigger Greater Profits

CLAIM 500 MORE POWER PHRASES!

Thank you for purchasing this eBook and in doing so we would like to send you **500 More Red Hot Power Phrases for FREE!**

When you post a **positive review of this Book on Amazon Books** under this title you'll receive an additional **500 POWER PHRASES**. Your review may also be sent directly to us.

Your request must be received within 30-days of purchase. Once your unbiased Book review is posted and verified, simply email the following to **(500@RIVOinc.com)**:

1. Full Name of Purchaser
2. Email address
3. Paypal Invoice Number
4. Copy of your posted Book Review*

Once we receive the above, we'll send you 500 Power Phrases **(PDF)** emailed to the address you provided.

Visit: www.RIVObooks.com for additional volumes as they become available including the Pro Edition of 5000 Red Hot Power Phrases that say what you mean to say and trigger greater profits.

Lynn and I look forward to your written comments and suggestions as we love hearing from each of our readers.

Richard & Lynn Voigt
RIVO Inc – RIVO Marketing
13720 West Keefe Avenue
Brookfield, Wisconsin 53005 USA
Telephone: (262) 783-5335
www.RIVObooks.com

P. S. If you love gardening, catch us on www.WisconsinGarden.com

*NOTE: This offer is valid providing it does not violate the terms of service of the entity with whom you made this purchase. Duplicate or incomplete entries will also not be eligible and this offer is limited to one request per email address. All eligible review submissions become the property of RIVO Inc - RIVO Marketing – RIVO books and may be used as promotional testimonials ads on RIVO Inc websites. This offer may be withdrawn at any time without prior written notice.